Copper Canyon Press
Broadside Register

Copper Canyon Press is in residence at Fort Worden State Park
in Port Townsend, Washington, under the auspices of Centrum.
Centrum is a gathering place for artists and creative thinkers
from around the world, students of all ages and backgrounds,
and audiences seeking extraordinary cultural enrichment.

First printing June 2017 | ISBN 978-1-55659-530-1

Copper Canyon Press
Post Office Box 271
Port Townsend, Washington 98368
www.coppercanyonpress.org

Signed, Limited Editions

Dear Reader,

Copper Canyon Press was founded in 1972 with a passion for poetry.

One place where that passion found expression was in letterpress broadsides—beautifully designed with hand-set type and ornaments, and printed in small runs on a Chandler & Price platen press.

These gorgeous pieces of literary ephemera came into the world for any number of reasons: to celebrate a book's release or mark a publishing milestone, to give as gifts to readers and donors, to distribute at readings and festivals.

Over the years we've taken special pleasure in finding our broadsides displayed in bookstores, living rooms, libraries, and workplaces. They even found their way into special exhibits at the Seattle Art Museum and Multnomah County Library in Portland, Oregon. Washington State University holds examples of over 300 different Copper Canyon broadsides in their Special Collections Library. Best of all, we once traded broadsides for a much-needed plumbing repair!

In the mid-2000s, Copper Canyon began working with other letterpress printers, including Stern & Faye, lone goose press, Expedition Press, and The North Press. Most recently, Copper Canyon collaborated with the School for Visual Concepts in Seattle and The North Press to produce a portfolio of broadsides featuring poetry on the theme of water.

You hold in your hands an anthology of broadsides and prints which are currently available from our inventory. Many are signed by the poet. They all represent the remaining copies of limited editions. And once they're gone, they're gone... though, in all but a few cases, the poem on the broadside can always be found within the Copper Canyon book it calls home.

Happy reading!

 Copper Canyon Press

PS This catalog also contains information about the few copies of signed limited edition books in our inventory from W.S. Merwin, Richard Siken, Jim Harrison, Bill Porter/Red Pine, and Ted Kooser.

BROADSIDES

MARVIN BELL
Less Self

Throwing your voice is one of those things also.
They think it's you when it's not you.
They certainly thought it was me.
I was there when the one they thought me said yes.
And no.
I send my voice out under cover of darkness.
It is widely assumed that winter makes the pine tree stronger.
The greenest hours are those after midnight.
Green remains.

Marvin Bell   *Nightworks: Poems 1962–2000*

LESS SELF

THROWING your voice is one of those things also.
They think it's you when it's not you.
They certainly thought it was me.
I was there when the one they thought me said yes.
And no.
I send my voice out under cover of darkness.
It is widely assumed that winter makes the pine tree stronger.
The greenest hours are those after midnight.
Green remains.

Copper Canyon Press

Size	7" x 7.5"	Year	2001
Available stock	10 of 250	Printed By	Sam Hamill
	Signed		and Nellie Bridge
Price	$25		

MARVIN BELL
To Dorothy

You are not beautiful, exactly.
You are beautiful, inexactly.
You let a weed grow by the mulberry
and a mulberry grow by the house.
So close, in the personal quiet
of a windy night, it brushes the wall
and sweeps away the day till we sleep.

A child said it, and it seemed true:
"Things that are lost are all equal."
But it isn't true. If I lost you,
the air wouldn't move, nor the tree grow.
Someone would pull the weed, my flower.
The quiet wouldn't be yours. If I lost you,
I'd have to ask the grass to let me sleep.

To Dorothy

Dorothy

Marvin Bell

From Marvin Bell's collection,
Nightworks: Poems 1962–2000.
Published by Copper Canyon Press,
a nonprofit publisher that believes
poetry is vital to language and living.

You are not beautiful, exactly.

You are beautiful, inexactly.

You let a weed grow by the mulberry

and a mulberry grow by the house.

So close, in the personal quiet

of a windy night, it brushes the wall

and sweeps away the day till we sleep.

A child said it, and it seemed true:

"Things that are lost are all equal."

But it isn't true. If I lost you,

the air wouldn't move, nor the tree grow.

Someone would pull the weed, my flower.

The quiet wouldn't be yours. If I lost you,

I'd have to ask the grass to let me sleep.

Size	9" x 6"	Year	2015
Available stock	50 of 250	Printed By	The North Press
Signed by Marvin Bell and Dorothy			
Price	$50		

OLGA BROUMAS
The Choir

I walk and I rest while the eyes of my dead
look through my own, inaudible
hosannas greet
the panorama charged serene
and almost ultraviolet with so much witness
Holy the sea, the palpitating membrane
divided into dazzling fields and whaledark by the sea.
Holy the dark, pierced by late revelers and dawnbirds,
the garbage truck suspended in shy light,
the oystershell and crushed clam of the driveway,
the dahlia pressed like lotus on its open palm.
Holy the handmade and created side by side,
the sapphire of their marriage,
green flies and shit and condoms in the crabshell
rinsed by the buzzing tide.
Holy the light—
the poison ivy livid in its glare,
the gypsy moths festooning the pine barrens,
the mating monarch butterflies between the chic boutiques.
The mermaid's handprint on the artificial reef. Holy the we,
cast in the mermaid's image, smooth crotch of mystery and scale,
inscrutable until divulged by god
and sex into its gender, every touch
a secret intercourse with angels as we walk
proffered and taken. Their great wings
batter the air, our retinas bloom silver spots like beacons.
Better than silicone or graphite flesh absorbs
the shock of the divine crash-landing.
I roll my eyes back, skylights brushed by plumage of detail,
the unrehearsed and minuscule, the anecdotal midnight
themes of the carbon sea where we are joined:
zinnia, tomato, garlic wreaths
crowning the compost heap.

THE CHOIR

I walk and I rest while the eyes of my dead
look through my own, inaudible
hosannas greet
the panorama charged serene
and almost ultraviolet with so much witness.
Holy the sea, the palpitating membrane
divided into dazzling fields and whaledark by the sun.
Holy the dark, pierced by late revelers and dawnbirds,
the garbage truck suspended in shy light,
the oystershell and crushed clam of the driveway,
the dahlia pressed like lotus on its open palm.
Holy the handmade and created side by side,
the sapphire of their marriage,
green flies and shit and condoms in the crabshell
rinsed by the buzzing tide.
Holy the light—
the poison ivy livid in its glare,
the gypsy moths festooning the pine barrens,
the mating monarch butterflies between the chic boutiques.
The mermaid's handprint on the artificial reef. Holy the we,
cast in the mermaid's image, smooth crotch of mystery and scale,
inscrutable until divulged by god
and sex into its gender, every touch
a secret intercourse with angels as we walk
proffered and taken. Their great wings
batter the air, our retinas bloom silver spots like beacons.
Better than silicone or graphite flesh absorbs
the shock of the divine crash-landing.
I roll my eyes back, skylights brushed by plumage of detail,
the unrehearsed and minuscule, the anecdotal midnight
themes of the carbon sea where we are joined:
zinnia, tomato, garlic wreaths
crowning the compost heap.

OLGA BROUMAS

 One hundred copies designed and printed by Sam Hamill
for the Copper Canyon Press board and staff retreat, 2000.

Size	7.25" x 13"	Year	2000
Available stock	10 of 100	Printed By	Sam Hamill
	Signed		
Price	$20		

STEPHEN BERG
from *Crow with No Mouth: Ikkyū*

this ink painting of wind blowing through pines
who hears it?

clouds very high look
not one word helped them get up there

alone with the icy moon no passion
these trees this mountain nothing else

nobody understands why we do what we do
this cup of *sake* does

passion's red thread is infinite
like the earth always under me

Crow with No Mouth: Ikkyu

this ink painting of wind blowing through pines
who hears it?

clouds very high look
not one word helped them get up there

alone with the icy moon no passion
these trees this mountain nothing else

nobody understands why we do what we do
this cup of *sake* does

passion's red thread is infinite
like the earth always under me

— *versions by Stephen Berg*

Three hundred copies designed and printed by Sam Hamill, Nellie Bridge, and Kathie Meyer, February, 2001, at Copper Canyon Press.

Size	9" x 10"	Year	2001
Available stock	50 of 300	Printed By	Sam Hamill
Price	$20		Nellie Bridge
			Kathie Meyer

HAYDEN CARRUTH
Her Song

She sings the blues in a voice that is partly
Irish. But "music is international." Singing
With her blue eyes open, her auburn hair
Flung back, yes, searching a distant horizon
For a sometime beacon or the first glimmer
Of sunrise. She sings in the dark. Only her own light
Illuminates her, although in the shadows
Are dim shapes, motionless, known to be
The tormented—in the bogs of Ireland, in
The bayous of Louisiana, relics of thousands
Upon thousands who suffered unimaginably
In ancient times. And in her husky contralto
They are suffering still. Knowingly she sings.
Music is anthropological. This is a burden,
For in her song no one can be redeemed.

hayden carruth

her song

she sings the blues in a voice that is partly
Irish. But "music is international." Singing
With her blue eyes open, her auburn hair
Flung back, yes, searching a distant horizon
For a sometime beacon or the first glimmer
Of sunrise. She sings in the dark. Only her own light
Illuminates her, although in the shadows
Are dim shapes, motionless, known to be
The tormented—in the bogs of Ireland, in
The bayous of Louisiana, relics of thousands
Upon thousands who suffered unimaginably
In ancient times. And in her husky contralto
They are suffering still. Knowingly she sings.
Music is anthropological. This is a burden,
For in her song no one can be redeemed.

Three hundred copies designed and printed by Sam Hamill,
Nellie Bridge, and Amy Schaus, in August, 2001,
celebrating publication of *Doctor Jazz*,
on the poet's 80th birthday.

Size	9.75" x 13.5"	Year	2001
Available stock	50⁺ of 300	Printed By	Sam Hamill
Price	$25		Nellie Bridge
			Amy Schaus

MADELINE DeFREES
The Register

All night I hear the one-way door sigh outward
into billboard glare. The ninth-floor
cul-de-sac left by the wrecker's ball, my new
apartment.

      Inside the known hotel, decor of watered
silk and fleur-de-lis, the French Provincial
red-and-white, mine for the night, no more. A weak
bulb wears a halo through the dark.

                  The street
divides below the skid of rubber burning. One branch
leads to a hill's last word, one into morning.
Flying in place, hung form its thirst, hummingbird
in the honey throat of a flower.

          Bless me,
Father, I have sins to spare and love
these relics of the hybrid years I spent afraid
to move. Chant of common life, field lilies, all
that labor, too cautious then to spin.
Not even Solomon would know these regal lily flowers,
translated fleur-de-lis my wall
provides, the glory flowers-*de-luce*, of light breaking
clean on the iris. I open
my eyes to the light.

        Bless me, Father,
under heavy sun and hoping
still to make your life my own. I cannot nullify
the work this body's done
nor call each act religion. Wherever one road
joins another, blind, I think of you
and conjure up the loss. When two roads, gaining
speed, speed up to intersect, I cross
myself and lay the body down, arms open for what comes
to pass. Father, I am signing in.

THE REGISTER

ALL night I hear the one-way door sigh outward
into billboard glare. The ninth-floor
cul-de-sac left by the wrecker's ball, my new
apartment.

Inside the known hotel, décor of watered
silk and fleur-de-lis, the French Provincial
red-and-white, mine for the night, no more. A weak
bulb wears a halo through the dark.

The street
divides below the skid of rubber burning. One branch
leads to a hill's last word, one into morning.
Flying in place, hung from its thirst, hummingbird
in the honey throat of a flower.

Bless me,
Father, I have sins to spare and love
these relics of the hybrid years I spent afraid
to move. Chant of common life, field lilies, all
that labor, too cautious then to spin.
Not even Solomon would know these regal lily flowers,
translated fleur-de-lis my wall
provides, the glory flowers-*de-luce*, of light breaking
clean on the iris. I open
my eyes to the light.

Bless me, Father,
under heavy sun and hoping
still to make your life my own. I cannot nullify
the work this body's done
nor call each act religion. Wherever one road
joins another, blind, I think of you
and conjure up the loss. When two roads, gaining
speed, speed up to intersect. I cross
myself and lay the body down, arms open for what comes
to pass. Father, I am signing in.

✤ *Madeline DeFrees*

Size	7.5" x 13"	Year	1980
Available stock	20 of 250	Printed By	Copper Canyon
Price	$20		Press

NORMAN DUBIE
The Amulet

for Laura

Blackbirds are scribbling in the winter heat of the trees.
You are accompanying reindeer over frozen water, a large cow
Collapses along a rising incline of rotten ice
With hundreds of animals now both quick and shy,
Pushing you over into the pine woods
And then nearly into a darkening sky.

But the moon is lowering its threads, lucent with fat,
Into this dream you are sinking with,
And here among the night fires you begin to worry

That the one moon passing like a needle through
The dreams of so many will no longer
Carry a sun. The cold dogs are barking.
You said that you woke, that you were both hungry and naked.

Then, you said, did I wake you? I'm sorry
If I did.

for Laura

Blackbirds are scribbling in the winter heat of the trees.
You are accompanying reindeer over frozen water, a large cow
Collapses along a rising incline of rotten ice
With hundreds of animals, now both quick and shy,
Pushing you over into the pine woods
And then nearly into a darkening sky.

But the moon is lowering its threads, lucent with fat,
Into this dream you are sinking with,
And here among the night fires you begin to worry

That the one moon passing like a needle through
The dreams of so many will no longer
Carry a sun. The cold dogs are barking.
You said that you woke, that you were both hungry and naked.

Then, you said, did I wake you? I'm sorry
If I did.

NORMAN DUBIE

Three hundred copies designed and printed at Copper Canyon Press by Sam Hamill, Nellie Bridge, and Susan Scarlata, March, 2001, celebrating the publication of The Mercy Seat: Collected and New Poems, 1967 – 2000.

Size	9" x 11.25"	Year	2001
Available stock	20 of 300	Printed By	Sam Hamill
	Signed		Nellie Bridge
Price	$25		Susan Scarlata

DAN GERBER
Six Kinds of Gratitude

(1)

I'm someone's small boat,
far out at sea,
sailing from what has so long sustained me
toward what I don't know.

My joy is the sound
of the water purling around me,
but is it my hull
or the great ocean moving?

(2)

Are those flies I hear, or a trick of the wind,
faintly human voices,
or a whistle of breath
in the nose of my sleeping dog?

(3)

Without *me* there is no confusion.
Buddhas see no difference between
themselves and other; Angels,
between the living and the dead.

(4)

At last I've discovered
the secret of life:
If you don't leave
you can't come back.

(5)

Deep in the Earth there are pockets of light
that did not come from Heaven,
and yet they are the light of Heaven
deep inside the Earth

(6)

This bird is the birdness of a bird.

SIX KINDS OF GRATITUDE

(1)
I'm someone's small boat,
far out at sea,
sailing from what has so long sustained me
toward what I don't know.

My joy is the sound
of the water purling around me,
but is it my hull
or the great ocean moving?

(2)
Are those flies I hear, or a trick of the wind,
faintly human voices,
or a whistle of breath
in the nose of my sleeping dog?

(3)
Without *me* there is no confusion.
Buddhas see no difference between
themselves and others; Angels,
between the living and the dead.

(4)
At last I've discovered
the secret of life:
*If you don't leave
you can't come back.*

(5)
Deep in the Earth there are pockets of light
that did not come from Heaven,
and yet they are the light of Heaven
deep inside the Earth.

(6)
This bird is the birdness of a bird.

Dan Gerber

Dan Gerber

From *A Primer on Parallel Lives*, Copper Canyon Press, 2007.
Two hundred copies printed by Daniel Urban.

COPPER CANYON PRESS

Size	6.5" x 13"	Year	2007
Available stock	25 of 200	Printed By	Daniel Urban
	Signed		
Price	$25		

HAN-SHAN
translated by RED PINE

No. 82

Spring water is pure in an emerald stream
moonlight is white on Cold Mountain
silence thoughts and the spirit becomes clear
contemplate emptiness and world becomes still

HAN-SHAN

№ 82

碧澗泉水清　　Spring water is pure in an emerald stream
寒山月華白　　moonlight is white on Cold Mountain
默知神自明　　silence thoughts and the spirit becomes clear
觀空境逾寂　　contemplate emptiness and the world becomes still

[詩] *Red Pine*

From *Finding Them Gone: Visiting China's Poets of the Past,*
by Bill Porter/Red Pine, Published by Copper Canyon Press.

Printed at The North Press, Port Townsend, Washington.

Size	8" x 8"	Year	2015
Available stock	50+ Signed	Printed By	The North Press
Price	$30		

JIM HARRISON

Poetry at its best is the language your soul would speak if you could teach your soul to speak.

POETRY
at its best
is the language
your soul would speak
if you could teach your soul to speak.

— *Jim Harrison*

Size	9" x 6"	Year	2015
Available stock	50⁺ of 300 Signed	Printed By	The North Press
Price	$50		

ROBERT HEDIN
An Hour Ago

In the small dusty
Galaxy of the garden,

Where the hydrangeas
Are all bright blue

And bask like planets
In the morning light,

I could hear Bashō
Hard at work, hoeing.

AN HOUR AGO

In the small dusty
Galaxy of the garden,

Where the hydrangeas
Are all bright blue

And bask like planets
In the morning light,

I could hear Bashō
Hard at work, hoeing.

Robert Hedin

From *At the Great Door of Morning*, published by Copper Canyon Press
Printed at The North Press, Port Townsend, Washington

Size	6.25" x 10"	Year	2017
Available stock	50+ of 115 Signed	Printed By	The North Press
Price	$20		

ROBERT HEDIN
Field Notes

Every poem
is a small creation
myth.

The poet has only one tool
the voice
and it starts in silence.

Pry to the roots,
the old familiar dark,
to the sweet smell of peat and swamp water.

FIELD
NOTES

Every poem
    is a small creation
myth.

          The poet has only one tool
             the voice
       and it starts in silence.

Pry to the roots,
    the old familiar dark,
to the sweet smell of peat and swamp water.

Robert Hedin

COPPER CANYON PRESS

Size	7" x 7.5"	Year	2017
Available stock	50⁺ of 100 Signed	Printed By	The North Press
Price	$20		

JIM HEYNEN
Staying With Old People

I knew I'd like them
when I saw their old
black car—it's long

gentle dents said
something about kindness,
about how to meet

an adversary. Do you
suppose the greatest
kindness is thoughtless?

He gets up early
and makes tea. He takes
his false teeth from

a glass and refills it
with warm water. Her teeth
are still in there,

warming up. When she
comes, those warm
teeth slide

into her warm mouth
so easily she hardly
notices her own smile.

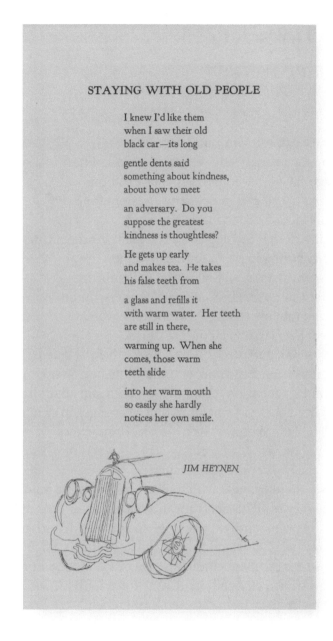

STAYING WITH OLD PEOPLE

I knew I'd like them
when I saw their old
black car—its long

gentle dents said
something about kindness,
about how to meet

an adversary. Do you
suppose the greatest
kindness is thoughtless?

He gets up early
and makes tea. He takes
his false teeth from

a glass and refills it
with warm water. Her teeth
are still in there,

warming up. When she
comes, those warm
teeth slide

into her warm mouth
so easily she hardly
notices her own smile.

JIM HEYNEN

Size	5.75" x 11.5"	Year	1981
Available stock	5 of 175	Printed By	Copper Canyon
Price	$20		Press

CAROLYN KIZER
Union of Women

At a literary gathering in Santa Monica
I encounter a bearded lady wearing a union button.
We engage each other in friendly conversation:
When I was a little girl in Spokane, Washington,
I took enormous satisfaction in the label
Sewn to my clothes by the Ladies Garment Workers Union.
I was contributing to the Wealth of Women
As I chose my dresses. O Solidarity! O Feminism!
Much later I met a Ladies Garment Workers Union
Leader who told me that she was the only woman
Who'd ever been an official in that union,
Always ignored, outvoted. I felt retrospectively cheated.
Now my new friend, the one with the white beard (she
Won't mind if I mention it, she wrote a cinquain about it)
Says that her Local 814 (mostly women) engages in struggle
With the terrible Sheraton, its unfair labor practices
Concerning the ladies who change the beds and mop the bathroom
And fold the ends of the toilet paper
Into those stupid triangles, and put the mints on the pillow.
Of course they're all blacks (I mean African American)
Or Mexicans who hardly speak English and fear deportation.
It's clear my bearded friend though old and lame is a fighter;
And she writes excellent cinquains: she just sent me a bunch.
(You know what a cinquain is? A nifty form in five lines
Adapted by Crapsey from the medieval French.)
She, as the current jargon has it, made my day.
So here's to Solidarity, cinquains, brave bearded ladies—Hooray!

union of women

AT A LITERARY gathering in Santa Monica
I encounter a bearded lady wearing a union button.
We engage each other in friendly conversation:
When I was a little girl in Spokane, Washington,
I took enormous satisfaction in the label
Sewn to my clothes by the Ladies Garment Workers Union.
I was contributing to the Wealth of Women
As I chose my dresses. O Solidarity! O Feminism!
Much later I met a Ladies Garment Workers Union
Leader who told me that she was the only woman
Who'd ever been an official in that union,
Always ignored, outvoted. I felt retrospectively cheated.
Now my new friend, the one with the white beard (she
Won't mind if I mention it, she wrote a cinquain about it)
Says that her Local 814 (mostly women) engages in struggle
With the terrible Sheraton, its unfair labor practices
Concerning the ladies who change the beds and mop the bathrooms,
And fold the ends of the toilet paper
Into those stupid triangles, and put the mints on the pillow.
Of course they're all blacks (I mean African Americans)
Or Mexicans who hardly speak English and fear deportation.
It's clear my bearded friend though old and lame is a fighter;
And she writes excellent cinquains: she just sent me a bunch.
(You know what a cinquain is? A nifty form in five lines
Adapted by Crapsey from the medieval French.)
She, as the current jargon has it, made my day.
So here's to Solidarity, cinquains, brave bearded ladies—Hooray!

Carolyn Kizer

*Two hundred copies designed and printed, hors de commerce,
by Sam Hamill and Leslie Cox, December, 2003, celebrating
the eightieth anniversary of the birth of the poet.*

Size	8" x 14"	Year	2003
Available stock	50+ of 200	Printed By	Sam Hamill
Price	$20		Leslie Cox

LU MEI-P'O
translated by RED PINE
The Snow And The Plum

The plum without the snow isn't very special
and snow without a poem is simply commonplace
at sunset when the poem is done then it snows again
together with the plum they complete the spring

THE SNOW AND THE PLUM

The plum without the snow isn't very special
and snow without a poem is simply commonplace
at sunset when the poem is done then it snows again
together with the plum they complete the spring

LU MEI-P'O

Three hundred copies of this broadside were designed and printed by Sam Hamill and
Leslie Cox, with calligraphy by Chungliang Al Huang. The poem is reprinted from
Poems of the Masters, translated by Red Pine, published by Copper Canyon Press.

Red Pine

Size	11.5" x 7"	Year	2004
Available stock	10 of 300	Printed By	Sam Hamill
	Signed		Leslie Cox
Price	$50		

THOMAS MCGRATH
from *Letter to an Imaginary Friend*

Dakota is everywhere.
                        A condition
                                    And I am only a device of memory
To call forth into this Present the flowering dead and the living
To enter the labyrinth and blaze the trail for the enduring journey
Toward the round dance and commune of light…
                                    to dive through the night of rock
(In which the statues of heroes sleep) beyond history to Origin
To build that legend where all journeys are one
                                                where identity
Exists
        where speech becomes song

THOMAS McGRATH

from LETTER TO AN IMAGINARY FRIEND

Dakota is everywhere.
                          A condition.
                                        And I am only a device of memory
To call forth into this Present the flowering dead and the living
To enter the labyrinth and blaze the trail for the enduring journey
Toward the round dance and commune of light…
                                        to dive through the night of rock
(In which the statues of heroes sleep) beyond history to Origin
To build that legend where all journeys are one
                                        where Identity
Exists
          where speech becomes song

Two hundred fifty copies designed and printed for friends of the press, summer, 1997.

COPPER CANYON PRESS

Size	9.5" x 14"	Year	1997
Available stock	50+ of 250	Printed By	Sam Hamill
Price	$35		

MEI YUAN
Falling Leaves

These autumn leaves are like old men:
huddled, doting on the dregs of day.

One frost, and they'll all come falling.
Some will come soon, the others later.

Falling Leaves

These autumn leaves are like old men:
huddled, doting on the dregs of day.

One frost, and they'll all come falling.
Some will come soon, the others later.

 Two hundred fifty copies reprinted from *I Don't Bow to Buddhas:*
Selected Poems of Yüan Mei, translated by J. P. Seaton, published
by Copper Canyon Press, 1997.

Size	7.25" x 8"	Year	1997
Available stock	25 of 250	Printed By	Sam Hamill
Price	$30		

W.S. MERWIN
West Wall

In the unmade light I can see the world
as the leaves brighten I see the air
the shadows melt and the apricots appear
now that the branches vanish I see the apricots
from a thousand trees ripening in the air
they are ripening in the sun along the west wall
apricots beyond number are ripening in the daylight

Whatever was there
I never saw those apricots swaying in the light
I might have stood in orchards forever
without beholding the day in the apricots
or knowing the ripeness of the lucid air
or touching the apricots in your skin
or tasking in your mouth the sun in the apricots

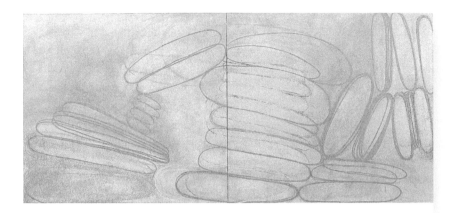

West Wall

—W.S. MERWIN

In the unmade light I can see the world
as the leaves brighten I see the air
the shadows melt and the apricots appear
now that the branches vanish I see the apricots
from a thousand trees ripening in the air
they are ripening in the sun along the west wall
apricots beyond number are ripening in the daylight

Whatever was there
I never saw those apricots swaying in the light
I might have stood in orchards forever
without beholding the day in the apricots
or knowing the ripeness of the lucid air
or touching the apricots in your skin
or tasting in your mouth the sun in the apricots

A limited edition broadside from Copper Canyon Press,
Port Townsend, Washington, 2012.
Poem from *Migration: New & Selected Poems* by W.S. Merwin
Art: Jill Moser, *Tender Ransom*, 2003, oil on canvas, 68 × 140 inches.

Size	8.5" x 11"	Year	2012
Available stock	10 of 250	Commercially printed	
Price	$25		

JANE MILLER
New Year's Stations
Station 8

A family of three
weary pilgrims hurrying
to their night's lodging—
a number of fires around
means a good harvest this year

STATION 8

A family of three
weary pilgrims hurrying
to their night's lodging—
a number of fires around
means a good harvest this year

JANE MILLER

Five hundred copies designed and printed by Sam Hamill
at winter solstice, 1999, for friends of the press.

Size	5.5" x 7.25"	Year	1999
Available stock	10 of 500	Printed By	Sam Hamill
Price	$20		

PABLO NERUDA
But if You Stretch Out Your Body

But if you stretch out your body, suddenly in the lugubrious shadow,
your blood upwells into the river of time and I hear
the whole sky cascading over my love
and you're part of the wildfire that sparks my whole lineage,
grant me then, by your golden life, the branch I've needed,
the flower that directs and sustains us,
the wheat that dies into bread and portions out our lives,
the mud with the smoothest fingers in the world,
the trains that whistle through frenzied cities,
the cluster of gillyflowers, the weight of gold inside the earth,
the froth born and dying behind the boat and the wing
of a gull that flies through the curling wave as though it were a bell tower.

Por eso si extiendes tu cuerpo y de pronto en la sombra sombría
asciende tu sangre en el río del tiempo y escucho
que pasa a través de mi amor la cascada del cielo
y que tú formas parte del fuego que corre escribiendo mi genealogía
me otorgue tu vida dorada la rama que necesitaba,
la flor que dirige las vidas y las continúa,
el trigo que muere en el pan y reparto la vida,
el barro que tiene los dedos más suaves del mundo,
los trenes que silban a través de ciudades salvajes,
el monte de los alhelíes, el peso del oro en la tierra,
la espuma que sigue al navío naciendo y muriendo y el ala
del ave marina que vuela en la ola como en un campanario.

But if you stretch out your body, suddenly in the lugubrious shadow,
your blood upwells into the river of time and I hear
the whole sky cascading over my love
and you're part of the wildfire that sparks my whole lineage,
grant me then, by your golden life, the branch I've needed,
the flower that directs and sustains us,
the wheat that dies into bread and portions out our lives,
the mud with the smoothest fingers in the world,
the trains that whistle through frenzied cities,
the cluster of gillyflowers, the weight of gold inside the earth,
the froth born and dying behind the boat and the wing
of a gull that flies through the curling wave as though it were a bell tower.

Translated by Forrest Gander

From *Then Come Back: The Lost Neruda*, published by
COPPER CANYON PRESS

Printed at The North Press, Port Townsend, Washington

Size	8" x 13"	Year	2016
Available stock	50+ of 200	Printed By	The North Press
Price	$35		

PABLO NERUDA
Crossing the Sky

Crossing the sky I near
the red ray of your hair.
Of earth and wheat I am and as I close in
your fire kindles itself
inside me and the rocks
and flour ignite.
That's why my heart
expands and rises
into bread for your mouth to devour,
and my blood is wine poured for you.
You and I are the land full of fruit.
Bread, fire, blood, and wine
make up the earthly love that sears us.

Por el cielo me acerco

al rayo rojo de tu cabellera.

De tierra y trigo soy y al acercarme

tu fuego se prepara

dentro de mí y enciende

las piedras y la harina.

Por eso crece y sube

mi corazón haciéndose

pan para que tu boca lo devore,

y mi sangre es el vino que te aguarda.

tú y yo somos la tierra con sus frutos.

Pan, fuego, sangre y vino

es el terrestre amor que nos abrasa.

*C*rossing the sky I near
the red ray of your hair.
Of earth and wheat I am and as I close in
your fire kindles itself
inside me and the rocks
and flour ignite.
That's why my heart
expands and rises
into bread for your mouth to devour,
and my blood is wine poured for you.
You and I are the land full of fruit.
Bread, fire, blood, and wine
make up the earthly love that sears us.

Translated by Forrest Gander

PABLO *Neruda*

From *Then Come Back: The Lost Neruda*, published by
COPPER CANYON PRESS

Designed at The North Press, Port Townsend, Washington

Size	9" x 12"	Year	2016
Available stock	25 of 200	Printed By	The North Press
Price	$25		

PABLO NERUDA
Por el cielo...

Por el cielo me acerco
al rayo rojo de tu cabellera.
De tierra y trigo soy y al acercarme
tu fuego se prepara
dentro de mí y enciende
las piedras y la harina.
Por eso crece y sube
mi corazón haciéndose
pan para que tu boca lo devore,
y mi sangre es el vino que te aguarda.
Tú y yo somos la tierra con sus frutos.
Pan, fuego, sangre y vino
es el terrestre amor que nos abrasa.

Lima 20 Diciembre 1952
11 de la mañana
volando a 3.500 mts
de altura entre
Recife y Rio Janeiro

MENU

Por el cielo me acerco
al rayo rojo de tu cabellera.
De tierra y trigo soy y al acercarme
tu fuego se prepara
dentro de mí y enciende
las piedras y la harina.
Por eso crece y sube
mi corazón haciéndose
pan para que tu boca lo devore.
Y mi sangre es el vino que te
aguarda.
Tú y yo somos la tierra con
sus frutos.
Pan, fuego, sangre y vino
es el terrestre amor que nos
abrasa.

Pablo Neruda

Size	9" x 12"	Year	2016
Available stock	25	Commercially printed	
Price	$20		

PABLO NERUDA
I Remember

I remember
and we rushed
through various streets
to find
bread,
dazzling
bottles,
a piece
of turkey,
some lemons,
one branch
in bloom
as on
that
flowery
day
when
from the ship,
encircled
by the dark
blue of a sacred sea,
your tiny
feet brought you
descending
step by step
to my heart,
and the bread, the flowers
the standup
choir
of noon,
a sea wasp
over the orange blossoms,
all of that

recuerdo,	I remember,
y recorrimos	and we rushed
otras calles	through various streets
buscando	to find
pan,	bread,
botellas	dazzling
deslumbrantes,	bottles,
un fragmento	a piece
de pavo,	of turkey,
unos limones,	some lemons,
una	one
rama	branch
en flor	in bloom
como	as on
aquel	that
día	flowery
florido	day
cuando	when
del barco,	from the ship,
rodeada	encircled
por el oscuro	by the dark
azul del mar sagrado	blue of a sacred sea,
tus menudos	your tiny
pies te trajeron	feet brought you
bajando	descending
grada y grada	step by step
hasta mi corazón,	to my heart,
y el pan, las flores	and the bread, the flowers
el coro	the standup
vertical	choir
del mediodía,	of noon,
una abeja marina	a sea wasp
sobre los azahares,	over the orange blossoms,
todo aquello	all of that

Translated by Forrest Gander

From *Then Come Back: The Lost Neruda*, published by

詩 COPPER CANYON PRESS

Printed at The North Press, Port Townsend, Washington

Size	8" x 13"	Year	2016
Available stock	50 of 200	Printed By	The North Press
Price	$35		

PABLO NERUDA
Lilac Leaves

Lilac
leaves
all the leaves,
explosion
of foliage,
the earth's
trembling
canopy,
cypresses that cleave the air,
whispers of oak,
grass
borne by the wind,
emotive poplar groves,
leaves of eucalyptus
with the contours of
blood-gorged moons,
leaves,
lips and eyelids,
mouths, eyes, the hair
of the earth,
in the sand
barely
a drop falls,
treetops brimming
with birdsong,
black chestnut,
last
to summon
sap and hoist it up,
magnolias and pines,
intense scents,
fresh
apples shivering

Hojas	Lilac
de lila	leaves
todas las hojas,	all the leaves,
multitud	explosion
del follaje,	of foliage,
pabellón	the earth's
tembloroso	trembling
de la tierra,	canopy,
ciprés que clava el aire,	cypresses that cleave the air,
rumores de la encina,	whispers of oak,
hierba	grass
que trajo el viento,	borne by the wind,
sensibles alamedas,	emotive poplar groves,
hojas de eucaliptus	leaves of eucalyptus
curvas como	with the contours of
lunas ensangrentadas,	blood-gorged moons,
hojas,	leaves,
labios y párpados,	lips and eyelids,
bocas, ojos, cabellos	mouths, eyes, the hair
de la tierra,	of the earth,
apenas	in the sand
en la arena	barely
cae	a drop
una gota	falls,
copas	treetops brimming
del trino,	with birdsong,
castaño negro,	black chestnut,
último	last
en recoger	to summon
la savia y levantarla,	sap and hoist it up,
magnolias y pinares,	magnolias and pines,
duros de aroma,	intense scents,
frescos	fresh
manzanos temblorosos	apples shivering

Translated by Forrest Gander

From *Then Come Back: The Lost Neruda*, published by
COPPER CANYON PRESS

Printed at The North Press, Port Townsend, Washington

Size	8" x 13"	Year	2016
Available stock	50 of 200	Printed By	The North Press
Price	$35		

BILL O'DALY
The Legacy

Grandfather, these inland hills
and the canyons we blasted with .225
shrink in the August sun.
The housing tracts put a stop
to our bullets; now at night
modern streetlights climb
like the edge of waves
over once sage-crowded slopes.
The wind embroiders *Vista del Mar*
in the dirt, across the yards
with their hacienda facades.
Hawks are fewer; they circle the bones
of banks under construction,
the air-conditioned curios
with "Country" in their names.
But on the ridge the cottage you built
with family hands and pine
has sold and sold again,
has sold and sold again,
has grown to twice its size. The blooming
prickly pear out back followed suit,
and the narrow canyon boulders
bear the scars of all our bullets,
and the winds call us home
across the forgotten streambed
we never meant to own.

BILL O'DALY

THE LEGACY

GRANDFATHER, these inland hills
and the canyons we blasted with .22s
shrink in the August sun.
The housing tracts put a stop
to our bullets; now at night
modern streetlights climb
like the edge of waves
over once sage-crowded slopes.
The wind embroiders *Vista del Mar*
in the dirt, across the yards
with their hacienda facades.
Hawks are fewer; they circle the bones
of banks under construction,
the air-conditioned curios
with "Country" in their names.
But on the ridge the cottage you built
with family hands and pine
has sold and sold again,
has grown to twice its size. The blooming
prickly pear out back followed suit,
and the narrow canyon boulders
bear the scars of all our bullets,
and the winds call us home
across the forgotten streambed
we never meant to own.

Size	7.5" x 12.5"	Year	2007
Available stock	10	Printed By	Sam Hamill
Price	$20		

GREGORY ORR
Orpheus & Eurydice

When Eurydice saw him
huddled in a thick cloak,
she should have known
he was alive,
the way he shivered
beneath its useless folds.

But what she saw
was the usual: a stranger
confused in a new world.
And when she touched him
on the shoulder,
it was nothing
personal, a kindness
he misunderstood.
To guide someone
through the halls of hell
is not the same as love.

Gregory Orr (signature)

ORPHEUS & EURYDICE

from a lyric sequence by
GREGORY ORR

When Eurydice saw him
huddled in a thick cloak,
she should have known
he was alive,
the way he shivered
beneath its useless folds.

But what she saw
was the usual: a stranger
confused in a new world.
And when she touched him
on the shoulder,
it was nothing
personal, a kindness
he misunderstood.
To guide someone
through the halls of hell
is not the same as love.

Two hundred fifty copies of this broadside were designed and printed by
Sam Hamill, Nellie Bridge, and Kathie Meyer, using hand set Lutetia,
Hadriano Stonecut, and Italian Old Style types on Arches
paper, and signed by the poet.

COPPER CANYON PRESS

Size	7.25" x 10"	Year	2001
Available stock	10 of 250	Printed By	Sam Hamill
	Signed		Nellie Bridge
Price	$20		Kathie Meyer

CAMILLE RANKINE
from *Matter in Retreat*

& what are we

to one another but a means
to a meaning we haven't yet

discovered two points of light
on the inky dark

& what
are
we

to one another but a means
to a meaning we haven't yet

discovered two points of light
on the inky dark

CAMILLE RANKINE

Size   7" x 10"   Year   2016
Available stock   50+   Printed By   Expedition Press
Price $20

KENNETH REXROTH
Another Spring

The seasons revolve and the years change
With no assistance or supervision
The moon, without taking thought,
Moves in its cycle, full, crescent, and full.

The white moon enters the heart of the river;
The air is drugged with azalea blossoms;
Deep in the night a pine cone fall;
our campfire dies out in the empty mountains.

The sharp stars flicker in the tree tremulous branches;
The lake is black, bottomless in the crystalline night;
High in the sky the Northern Crown
Is cut in half by the dim summit of a snow peak.

O heart, heart, so singularly
Intransigent and corruptible,
Here we lie entranced by the starlit water,
And moments that should each last forever

Slide unconsciously by us like water.

KENNETH REXROTH

ANOTHER SPRING

The seasons revolve and the years change
With no assistance or supervision.
The moon, without taking thought,
Moves in its cycle, full, crescent, and full.

The white moon enters the heart of the river;
The air is drugged with azalea blossoms;
Deep in the night a pine cone falls;
Our campfire dies out in the empty mountains.

The sharp stars flicker in the tremulous branches;
The lake is black, bottomless in the crystalline night;
High in the sky the Northern Crown
Is cut in half by the dim summit of a snow peak.

O heart, heart, so singularly
Intransigent and corruptible,
Here we lie entranced by the starlit water,
And moments that should each last forever

Slide unconsciously by us like water.

Size	11" x 14"	Year	2004
Available stock	50+ of 300	Printed By	Sam Hamill
Price	$20		Leslie Cox

ADRIENNE RICH
Equinox

Time split like a fruit between dark and light
and a usual fog drags
over this landfall
I've walked September end to end
barefoot room to room
carrying in hand a knife well-honed for cutting stem or root
                         or wick   eyes open
to abalone shells   memorial candle flames
split lemons roses laid
            along charring logs   Gorgeous things
: : dull acres of developed land as we had named it: Nowhere
wetland   burnt garbage looming at its heart
gun-metal thicket   midnightblue blood and
                  tricking masks   I though I knew
history was not a novel

So can I say it was not I   listed as Innocence
betrayed you   serving (and protesting always)
the motives of my government
thinking we'd scratch out a place
where poetry   old subversive shape
grew out of Nowhere, here?
where skin could lie on skin
a place "outside the limits"
                Can say I was mistaken?

To be so bruised: in the soft organs   skeins of
                consciousness
Over and over have let it be
damage to others   crushing of the animate core
that tone-deaf cutloose ego swarming the world
so bruised: heart   spleen   long inflamed ribbons
              of the guts
the spine's vertical necklace swaying

Have let it swarm
through us   let it happen
as it must, inmost

but before this   long before this   those other eyes
frontally exposed themselves and spoke

EQUINOX

ADRIENNE RICH

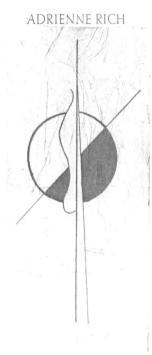

COPPER CANYON PRESS

Time split like a fruit between dark and light
and a usual fog drags
over this landfall
I've walked September end to end
barefoot room to room
carrying in hand a knife well-honed for cutting stem or root
                          or wick   eyes open
to abalone shells   memorial candle flames
split lemons roses laid
                along charring logs   Gorgeous things

: : dull acres of developed land as we had named it: Nowhere
wetland   burnt garbage looming at its heart
gun-metal thicket   midnightblue blood and
                  tricking masks   I thought I knew
history was not a novel

So can I say it was not I   listed as Innocence
betrayed you   serving (and protesting always)
the motives of my government
thinking we'd scratch out a place
where poetry   old subversive shape
grew out of Nowhere, here?
where skin could lie on skin
a place "outside the limits"

                        Can say I was mistaken?

To be so bruised: in the soft organs   skeins of
                        consciousness
Over and over have let it be
damage to others   crushing of the animate core
that tone-deaf cutloose ego swarming the world
so bruised: heart   spleen   long inflamed ribbons
                        of the guts
the spine's vertical necklace swaying

Have let it swarm
through us   let it happen
as it must, inmost

but before this   long before this   those other eyes
frontally exposed themselves and spoke

Size   9.5" x 14"   Year   2002
Available stock   20 of 300   Printed By   Sam Hamill
Price $50   Leslie Cox

THEODORE ROETHKE
from *On Poetry & Craft*

What we need is more people who specialize in the impossible

What we need is more people who

SPECIALIZE

IN THE ⁓ *Theodore Roethke*

IMPOSSIBLE

From *On Poetry & Craft*   published by Copper Canyon Press

Size	9" x 6"	Year	2015
Available stock	50$^+$ of 300	Printed By	The North Press
Price	$20		

REBECCA SEIFERLE
The Gift

I was wrong when I compared the mask of my own face
to an artifact, some kind of relic, or the shed skin of a snake.
That day there was no wounding. At the museum,
that morning, when the woman was teaching
the children how to make masks of their own faces
with the plaster of paris bandages that doctors use
for instant casts, I was glad to lather
my daughter's faces with lotion, to place the wet strips
on their faces, and later to feel on my own face,
the patting of their hands like the beating of eyelashes against
my cheeks. The fine grit of dissolved earth floating
on my own skin was pleasant, cool, and afterward, choosing
the colors to paint the mask was like selecting one's own
plumage: Ann's singular purple, Maria's
black-and-white splashed with orange, my turquoise.
When I was holding the shape of my own face in my hand,
it was nothing like a death mask. I saw how easy it was
to put the self aside and pick it up again. It wasn't the sacrificial mask
I'd seen in Mexico—a human skull inlaid with lapis lazuli, a
   merciless reduction—
but a moment of happiness, a fragile shell, the gift
of mother and daughters, when, laughing,
we shaped one another into being
by touching what we were.

[signature]

REBECCA SEIFERLE

the gift

I was wrong when I compared the mask of my own face
to an artifact, some kind of relic, or the shed skin of a snake.
That day, there was no wounding. At the museum,
that morning, when the woman was teaching
the children how to make masks of their own faces
with the plaster of paris bandages that docters use
for instant casts, I was glad to lather
my daughters' faces with lotion, to place the wet strips
on their faces, and later to feel on my own face,
the patting of their hands like the beating of eyelashes against
my cheeks. The fine grit of dissolved earth floating
on my skin was pleasant, cool, and, afterward, choosing
the colors to paint the mask was like selecting one's own
plumage: Ann's singular purple, Maria's
black-and-white splashed with orange, my turquoise.
When I was holding the shape of my own face in my hand,
it was nothing like a death mask. I saw how easy it was
to put the self aside and pick it up again. It wasn't the sacrificial mask
I'd seen in Mexico—a human skull inlaid with lapis lazuli, a
    merciless reduction—
but a moment of happiness, a fragile shell, the gift
of mother and daughters, when, laughing,
we shaped one another into being
by touching what we were.

Three hundred copies designed and printed by Sam Hamill and Daniel Urban
in the summer, 2001, and signed by the poet, celebrating the publication of
Bitters.

Size	7" x 13"	Year	2001
Available stock	50 of 300	Printed By	Sam Hamill
	Signed		Daniel Urban
Price	$20		

RICHARD SIKEN
from *Dots Everywhere*

It's nothing like I thought it
would be and closer to what I meant. *None of it is
real, darling.* I say it to you. Maybe we will wake up
singing.

It's nothing like I thought it
would be and

closer
to what
I meant.

Real, darling? None of it.
Maybe we will wake up
singing.

RICHARD SIKEN

Size	7" x 10"	Year	2015
Available stock	50	Printed By	Expedition Press
Price	$20		

FRANK STANFORD
Dreamt By A Man In A Field

I am thinking of the dead
Who are still with us.
They are not like us, they are
Young and beautiful,
On their way in the rain
To meet their lovers.
On their way with their dark umbrellas,
Always laughing, so quick,
Like limbs flying back
In a boat before night,
So constant,
Like the glass floats
The fishermen use in Japan.
But for them there is no moon,
For us the same news
We do not receive.

FRANK STANFORD

DREAMT BY A MAN
IN A FIELD

I am thinking of the dead
Who are still with us.
They are not like us, they are
Young and beautiful,
On their way in the rain
To meet their lovers.
On their way with their dark umbrellas,
Always laughing, so quick,
Like limbs flying back
In a boat before night,
So constant,
Like the glass floats
The fishermen use in Japan.
But for them there is no moon,
For us the same news
We do not receive.

From *What About This*, published by Copper Canyon Press
Printed at The North Press, Port Townsend, Washington

Size	8" x 9.25"	Year	2015
Available stock	25 of 50	Printed By	The North Press
Price	$35		

PRIMUS ST. JOHN
Ars Poetica

At the edge of the forest
In the middle of the darkness
There is a hand,
As cold as copper,
Like a river
Stretched over wide stones.
Despite the hard rocks
And the furious wind
I love hair
Like a flock of birds
Or a mild herd come to drink
For the exquisite rage
And sleek moss of her art.
There is something about a poem
That is violent
That is just another way to die,
Each time we realize our mysteries
We are weakened.
When I am writing I often scatter
Across a lascivious empire
Of passionate flowers.
They all seem so subversive
Even the ones with all their clothes on
They are so obsessed with the minute
Implication of who they are.
I believe if there is a struggle
It should go on
Where real lovers are.
I no longer regret
That I have smelted into one piece
For the sake of this poem.

PRIMUS ST. JOHN

ARS POETICA

At the edge of the forest
In the middle of the darkness
There is a hand,
As cold as copper.
Like a river
Stretched over wide stones.
Despite the hard rocks
And the furious wind
I love her
Like a flock of birds
Or a mild herd come to drink
For the exquisite rage
And sleek moss of her art.
There is something about a poem
That is violent
That is just another way to die,
Each time we realize our mysteries
We are weakened.
When I am writing I often scatter
Across a lascivious empire
Of passionate flowers.
They all seem so subversive
Even the ones with all their clothes on
They are so obsessed with the minute
Implication of who they are.
I believe if there is a struggle
It should go on
Where real lovers are.
I no longer regret
That I have smelted into one piece
For the sake of this poem.

 Two hundred copies printed at Copper Canyon Press
by Sam Hamill, B. J. Doty & Nellie Bridge,
July 21, 2000, celebrating the 62nd birthday of the poet.

Size	7.5" x 14"	Year	2000
Available stock	10 of 200	Printed By	Sam Hamill
Price	$20		Nellie Bridge
			B.J. Doty

RUTH STONE
One Thought

Accompanied
by many pictures,
the words
swelled and shrank.
The brain
flashed intermittently,
easily explained
in a simple collider.
The energy of nothing
smashed into the
energy of something.
There was complicity
in our smiles.
One thought—
I cannot live without you,
O brief and inconceivable other.

One Thought

Ruth Stone

From *What Love Comes To: New & Selected Poems*,
published by Copper Canyon Press
and printed by hand at The North Press,
Port Townsend, Washington.

Accompanied
by many pictures,
the words
swelled and shrank.
The brain
flashed intermittently,
easily explained
in a simple collider.
The energy of nothing
smashed into the
energy of something.
There was complicity
in our smiles.
One thought —
I cannot live without you,
O brief and inconceivable other.

Size	9" x 6"	Year	2013
Available stock	50	Printed By	The North Press
Price	$30		

STONEHOUSE
translated by RED PINE
from *The Mountain Poems of Stonehouse*

A hundred years slip by unnoticed
eighty-four thousand cares dissolve in stillness
a mountain image shimmers on sunlit water
snowflakes swirl above a glowing stove

綠水光中山影轉　百年日月閒中度　　八萬塵勞靜處消

紅爐焰上雪花飄

A hundred years slip by unnoticed
eighty-four thousand cares dissolve in stillness
a mountain image shimmers on sunlit water
snowflakes swirl above a glowing stove

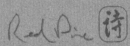

From *The Mountain Poems of Stonehouse*,
translated by Red Pine,
published by Copper Canyon Press.
Printed at The North Press, Port Townsend, Washington.

83/150

Size	9.5" x 9"	Year	2014
Available stock	50 of 150	Printed By	The North Press
	Signed		
Price	$40		

ARTHUR SZE
From a Painting of a Cat

Nan Ch'uan wanted to be reborn as a water buffalo,
but who did the body of the malicious cat become?
Black clouds and covering snow are alike.
It took thirty years for clouds to disperse, snow to melt.

PA-TA-SHAN-JEN

From a Painting of a Cat

Nan Ch'uan wanted to be reborn as a water buffalo,

but who did the body of the malicious cat become?

Black clouds and covering snow are alike.

It took thirty years for clouds to disperse, snow to melt.

A KAGE-AN BOOK FROM COPPER CANYON PRESS

Size	9.5" x 8.5"	Year	2001
Available stock	50 of 250	Printed By	Sam Hamill
	Signed		Nellie Bridge
Price	$25		

ELAINE TERRANOVA
Self-Examination

He might be tethered
like an animal, kept from where
he wants to be. A big man,
nearing sixty. He sits and sweats,
though the room is air-conditioned.
His mouth a little open, he is reading
the sign on the door marked Radiology.
He is half up to go after her,

thinking of this life
of hers. The lapses in the love—
his love—which cushions it.
The mutilating surgery and drugs
that sting the organism so it
draws back into itself, counterforce
to the disease. Whatever she has suffered
away from him in other rooms.

I pass easily where he
is not allowed. Like her, I'm chilled
in my thin gown. There is
a fineness, a definiteness
to her face. This beauty
is her own decision. A TV screen
plays a loop of film, women circling
their breasts with their finger tips,
women staring to a mirror.

A foam rubber breast is lying
on a table. Each of us takes it
in turn, like a lump of dough
we must knead smooth. Something solid
stops me. Unyielding, jewel-hard, a pebble
in this mud. Such seeds grow.
I touch the hollow between
my breasts, this emptiness
that is in me a sign of want.
I look at our still-dressed hands.
Watches, rings. What do they have
to do with us?—madly flashing in the light.

ELAINE TERRANOVA

Self-Examination

He might be tethered
like an animal, kept from where
he wants to be. A big man,
nearing sixty. He sits and sweats,
though the room is air-conditioned.
His mouth a little open, he is reading
the sign on the door marked Radiology.
He is half up to go after her,

thinking of this life
of hers. The lapses in the love —
his love — which cushions it.
The mutilating surgery and drugs
that sting the organism so it
draws back into itself, counterforce
to the disease. Whatever she has suffered
away from him in other rooms.

I pass easily where he
is not allowed. Like her, I'm chilled
in my thin gown. There is
a fineness, a definiteness
to her face. This beauty
is her own decision. A TV screen
plays a loop of film, women circling
their breasts with their fingertips,
women staring into a mirror.

A foam rubber breast is lying
on a table. Each of us takes it
in turn, like a lump of dough
we must knead smooth. Something solid
stops me. Unyielding, jewel-hard, a pebble
in this mud. Such seeds grow.
I touch the hollow between
my breasts, this emptiness
that is in me a sign of want.
I look at our still-dressed hands.
Watches, rings. What do they have
to do with us? — madly flashing in the light.

 from *Damages*, Copper Canyon Press, 1995

Size	7.5" x 13"	Year	1995
Available stock	10	Printed By	Copper Canyon
Price	$20		Press

JEAN VALENTINE
Great-Grandmother

be with us
as if in the one same day & night
we all gave birth
in the one same safe house, warm,
and then we rest together,
sleep, and nurse,
dreamily talk to our babies, warm
in a safe room   all of us
carried in the close black sky.

Great-grandmother

be with us
as if in the one same day & night
we all gave birth
in the one same safe house, warm,
and then we rest together,
sleep, and nurse,
dreamily talk to our babies, warm
in a safe room   all of us
carried in the close black sky.

J E A N   V A L E N T I N E

From *Shirt in Heaven*,
Published by Copper Canyon Press.

Printed at The North Press,
Port Townsend, Washington.

Size	8" x 10"	Year	2015
Available stock	50	Printed By	The North Press
Price	$35		

OCEAN VUONG
from *Someday I'll Love Ocean Vuong*

       The most beautiful part of your body
is where it's headed. And remember,
loneliness is still time spent
with the world.

The most beautiful part of your body
is where it's headed. & remember,
loneliness is still time spent
with the world.

OCEAN VUONG

From "Someday I'll Love Ocean Vuong," *Night Sky with Exit Wounds*
Copper Canyon Press, 2016 · Print by Expedition Press

Size	7" x 10"	Year	2016
Available stock	50	Printed By	Expedition Press
Price	$30		

REBECCA WEE
Pont Des Arts

She's bent in a posture of anguish or prayer
in a spot of city filth.

Head down, a stained knit cap
with its few coins on the ground beside her,
and her pliant child, a shadow.

Someone veers past with a friend
in a clamor of rings and scarves. A pretty child
skips after them, scattering pigeons.

The mothers miss how their daughters' eyes catch then—
the wary, openmouthed stares.

A terrible knowledge passes between them,
the bridge rippling under their feet

as the polished child rushes past but looks back
at the one on the bridge in the heat—

the sunblown silent one
whose hand has pulled back and flown up to smooth,
for a moment, her heavy hair.

REBECCA WEE

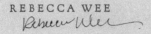

PONT DES ARTS

She's bent in a posture of anguish or prayer
in a spot of city filth.

Head down, a stained knit cap
with its few coins on the ground beside her,
and her pliant child, a shadow.

Someone veers past with a friend
in a clamor of rings and scarves. A pretty child
skips after them, scattering pigeons.

The mothers miss how their daughters' eyes catch then—
the wary, openmouthed stares.

A terrible knowledge passes between them,
the bridge rippling under their feet

as the polished child rushes past but looks back
at the one on the bridge in the heat—

the sunblown silent one
whose hand has pulled back and flown up to smooth,
for a moment, her heavy hair.

Three hundred copies designed and printed by Sam Hamill, Nellie Bridge,
and Amy Schaus, celebrating publication of Uncertain Grace *by*

COPPER CANYON PRESS

Size	7.5" x 11.75"	Year	2001
Available stock	50⁺ of 300	Printed By	Sam Hamill
	Signed		Nellie Bridge
Price	$20		Amy Schaus

JAMES WELCH
The Man From Washington

The end came easy for most of us.
Packed away in our crude beginnings
in some far corner of a flat world,
we didn't expect much more
than firewood and buffalo robes
to keep us warm. The man came down,
a slouching dwarf with rainwater eyes,
and spoke to us. He promised
that life would go on as usual,
that treaties would be signed, and everyone—
man, woman and child—would be inoculated
against a world in which we had no part,
a world of wealth, promise and fabulous disease.

THE MAN FROM WASHINGTON

The end came easy for most of us.
Packed away in our crude beginnings
in some far corner of a flat world,
we didn't expect much more
than firewood and buffalo robes
to keep us warm. The man came down,
a slouching dwarf with rainwater eyes,
and spoke to us. He promised
that life would go on as usual,
that treaties would be signed, and everyone---
man, woman and child--- would be inoculated
against a world in which we had no part,
a world of wealth, promise and fabulous disease.

James Welch

a Copperhead broadside

Size	8" x 13"	Year	1975
Available stock	10 of 150	Printed By	Copperhead
Price	$70		

KATHLEENE WEST
After Matchbox Funerals, Stock Trucks
& Elegies in the Pasture

Not many old animals on a farm. Sometimes
the watchdog's smart enough
not to chase machinery
or a prize cow tops the milk bucket
one more season. An occasional wily cat.
These earned their names
and I call them out:

> *Colonel Doberman*
> *Old Roan*
> *Gray Whiskers*

Each spring a farm bleats and squeals—impatient
with new animals,
I name as many as I can mark.
This year the orphaned pig is Joseph,
Rose Red, the delicate Guernsey heifer,
And Chicken Little, the timid Leghorn
that won't rush to the feeder.
I can't stop the baby chicks
from piling up in the corner
and smothering the one I meant to protect.
Between midnight and dawn,
a sow devours the runt.
The calf falls down on its knees.

Some lived long enough to recognize me,
ran on shaky legs
when I brandished the Nehi bottle of milk.
Converted to lamb chops & sausage,
they prospered the table.
Looking the other way,
I passed the platters of what used to be
Bobtail or Slurpy
and vowed I'd name nothing more
and care only for what grew in gardens.

It can't be helped,
Mother said.
Blizzards, floods, each animal death
can't be helped.
Twins one night.
You didn't know.
One born dead;
one already grown & thriving.
It can't be helped.
It's more than recognition
or your love
that makes the difference.

After Matchbox Funerals, Stock Trucks
& Elegies in the Pasture

Not many old animals on a farm. Sometimes
the watchdog's smart enough
not to chase machinery
or a prize cow tops the milk bucket
one more season. An occasional wily cat.
These earned their names
and I call them out:

Colonel Doberman
Old Roan
Gray Whiskers

Each spring a farm bleats and squeals—impatient
with new animals.
I name as many as I can mark.
This year the orphaned pig is Joseph.
Rose Red, the delicate Guernsey heifer.
And Chicken Little, the timid Leghorn
that won't rush to the feeder.
I can't stop the baby chicks
from piling up in the corner
and smothering the one I meant to protect.
Between midnight and dawn,
a sow devours the runt.
The calf falls down on its knees.

Some lived long enough to recognize me,
ran on shaky legs
when I brandished the Nehi bottle of milk.
Converted to lamb chops & sausage,
they prospered the table.
Looking the other way,
I passed the platters of what used to be
Bobtail or Slurpy
and vowed I'd name nothing more
and care only for what grew in gardens.

It can't be helped,
Mother said.
Blizzards, floods, each animal death
can't be helped.
Twins one night.
You didn't know.
One born dead;
one already grown & thriving.
It can't be helped.
It's more than recognition
or your love
that makes the difference.

 Kathleene West

Size   5" x 13"   Year   1978
Available stock   25   Printed By   Copper Canyon
Price $20   Press

KATHLEENE WEST
Roundel on a Sonnet by Marilyn Hacker

We need more boozy women poets,
I read. The whiskey blurs, confuses
me near enough to accepting it,
but first—we need more booze.

And then, define the crucial word. To booze:
drinking to excess, and there we've set
the standard to join our Muse
of bourbon-in-hand women poets, reciting sonnets

in colorful bars, and not just sonnets,
but bawdy pantoums and tough lyrics—to lose
"poetess" forever, but Hell—we don't need more poets
of any kind. We need more booze.

Roundel on a Sonnet by Marilyn Hacker

We need more boozy women poets,
I read. The whiskey blurs, confuses
me near enough to accepting it,
but first—we need more booze.

And then, define the crucial word. To booze:
drinking to excess, and there we've set
the standard to join our Muse
of bourbon-in-hand women poets, reciting sonnets

in colorful bars, and not just sonnets,
but bawdy pantoums and tough lyrics—to lose
"poetess" forever, but Hell—we don't need more poets
of any kind. We need more booze.

Kathleene West

Size	10" x 11"	Year	1977
Available stock	10	Printed By	Copper Canyon
Price	$20		Press

C.K. WILLIAMS
Lost Wax

My love gives me some wax,
so for once instead of words
I work at something real;
I knead until I see emerge
a person, a protagonist;
but I must overwork my wax,
it loses its resiliency,
comes apart in crumbs.

I take another block;
this work, I think, will be a self;
I can feel it forming, brow
and brain; perhaps it will be me,
perhaps, if I can create myself,
I'll be able to mend myself;
my wax, though, freezes
this time, fissures, splits.

Words or wax, no end
to our self-shaping, our forlorn
awareness at the end of which
is only more awareness.
Was ever truth so malleable?
Arid, inadhesive bits of matter.
What might heal you? Love.
What makes you whole? Love. My love.

Lost Wax

My love gives me some wax,
so for once instead of words
I work at something real;
I knead until I see emerge
a person, a protagonist;
but I must overwork my wax,
it loses its resiliency,
comes apart in crumbs.

I take another block:
this work, I think, will be a self;
I can feel it forming, brow
and brain; perhaps it will be me,
perhaps, if I can create myself,
I'll be able to mend myself;
my wax, though, freezes
this time, fissures, splits.

Words or wax, no end
to our self-shaping, our forlorn
awareness at the end of which
is only more awareness.
Was ever truth so malleable?
Arid, inadhesive bits of matter.
What might heal you? Love.
What make you whole? Love. My love.

—C.K. WILLIAMS

A limited edition broadside from Copper Canyon Press,
Port Townsend, Washington, 2012.
Poem from *Love About Love: Poems* by C.K. Williams
Art: Kevin Piepel, *Surfacing #17*, 2011, encaustic on panel,
24 × 18 inches. Courtesy Foster/White Gallery.

Size	8.5" x 11"	Year	2012
Available stock	10	Commercially printed	
Price	$20		

C.D. WRIGHT
It is a function of poetry...

It is a function of poetry to locate those zones inside us
that would be free, and declare them so.

would be free, and declare them so.

— C.D. Wright

● It is a function of poetry

that

inside us

to locate

those zones

COPPER CANYON PRESS • Printed at The North Press, Port Townsend, Washington

Size	9" x 6"	Year	2016
Available stock	50+	Printed By	The North Press
Price	$25		

DEAN YOUNG
Changing Genres

I was satisfied with haiku until I met you,
jar of octopus, cuckoo's cry, 5-7-5,
but now I want a Russian novel,
a 50-page description of you sleeping,
another 75 of what you think staring out
a window. I don't care about the plot
although I suppose there will have to be one,
the usual separation of the lovers, turbulent
seas, danger of decommission in spite
of constant war, time in gulps and glitches
passing, squibs of threnody, a fallen nest,
speckled eggs somehow uncrushed, the sled,
outracing the wolves on the steppes, the huge
glittering ball where all that matters
is a kiss at the end of a dark hall.
At dawn the officers ride back to the garrison,
one without a glove, the entire last chapter
about a necklace that couldn't be worn
inherited by a great-niece
along with the love letters bound in silk.

Changing Genres
Dean Young

From **BENDER**,
published by
Copper Canyon Press
and printed by hand
at **The North Press**,
Port Townsend,
Washington.

I was satisfied with haiku until I met you,
jar of octopus, cuckoo's cry, 5-7-5,
but now I want a Russian novel,
a 50-page description of you sleeping,
another 75 of what you think staring out
a window. I don't care about the plot
although I suppose there will have to be one,
the usual separation of the lovers, turbulent
seas, danger of decommission in spite
of constant war, time in gulps and glitches
passing, squibs of threnody, a fallen nest,
speckled eggs somehow uncrushed, the sled
outracing the wolves on the steppes, the huge
glittering ball where all that matters
is a kiss at the end of a dark hall.
At dawn the officers ride back to the garrison,
one without a glove, the entire last chapter
about a necklace that couldn't be worn
inherited by a great-niece
along with the love letters bound in silk.

Size	7" x 10"	Year	2016
Available stock	25	Printed By	The North Press
	Signed		
Price	$50		

Spinning Down
to Clear Water

This portfolio of letterpressed broadsides is the result of a collaboration between Copper Canyon Press and the School for Visual Concepts in Seattle. In the Spring of 2017, under the guidance of Ellie Mathews of The North Press, eight designers used handset type and photopolymer plates to create broadsides centered around the theme of water.

Portfolio includes the following broadsides:

Ted Kooser, *Dishwater*
Dan Gerber, *After the Rain*
Alberto Ríos, *The Thirst of Things*
Jim Harrison, *Waves*
Olav H. Hauge, *Ocean* (translated by Robert Hedin)
Heather Allen, *Pool*
Arthur Sze, *June Ghazal*
Tom Hennen, *Late March*

Available exclusively through donations of $100 or greater.

Spinning Down
to Clear Water

Choosing a theme for this suite of poems was easy: water. Selecting the poems, not so easy. A wealth of suggestions poured in. Ultimately, eight designers in a master class at the School of Visual Concepts in Seattle, spent an evening paging through books, reading aloud, discussing, and deciding which poems best fit our theme. We are thrilled with the results of that process, a balance of ocean, river, rain, and desert.

The poems were letterpress printed with handset type and photopolymer plates under the guidance of Ellie Mathews. We are grateful to Boxcar Press, Neenah Paper, and Washi Arts for their support.

LAURA BENTLEY   HEIDI HESPELT

CHRIS COPLEY   SUKMIE PATEL

DANIELLE CRANDALL   AMY REDMOND

GLENN FLEISHMAN   JANE SUCHAN

Copper Canyon Press
School of Visual Concepts
Spring 2017

Spinning Down
to Clear Water

COPPER CANYON PRESS

DISHWATER
TED KOOSER

Slap of the screen door, flat knock
   of my grandmother's boxy black shoes
      on the wooden stoop, the hush and sweep
        of her knob-kneed, cotton-aproned stride
         out to the edge and then, toed in
          with a furious twist and heave,
           a bridge that leaps from her hot red hands
           and hangs there shining for fifty years
         over the mystified chickens,
        over the swaying nettles, the ragweed,
      the clay slope down to the creek,
     over the redwing blackbirds in the tops
   of the willows, a glorious rainbow
with an empty dishpan swinging at one end.

From *Delights & Shadows*, published by Copper Canyon Press.
Designed and printed by Jane Suchan at the School of Visual Concepts, Seattle, Washington.

After the Rain

Dan Gerber

I SPOT a young barn owl
standing by the road
peering at his own reflection in a puddle,
or so it seems,
when I pull off on the shoulder to see
if I can help.

Dazed,
probably struck by a car,
though not visibly wounded,
he looks up across the puddle
where I'm standing,
as if to ask about this
wondrous, underground bird he is seeing,
as if to ask if I see it, too.

From *A Primer on Parallel Lives*, published by Copper Canyon Press.
Designed and printed by Glenn Fleishman at the School of Visual Concepts, Seattle, Washington.

ALBERTO RÍOS

THE THIRST OF THINGS

Desert having been ocean
Remembers water, misses it,

Hugs it and kisses it when it visits,
Steals a little when it tries to leave,

Prickly pear and ocotillo and mesquite
A little fatter, a little wider, a little greener,

These plants having been coral and puffer fish
And green seaweed in their ocean lives.

In this place now, one can still see
This place *then,*

Every grain of sand once having been
A point of light in the crest of a wave.

Heat on the highway, that slight, quivering
Ghost of the desert world,

That mirage shows for its brief moment
The fierce *what-was* in all of us.

From a broadside produced by Suzanne Vigil
in Copper Canyon Press, Designed and
printed by Arts Reunion at the School of
Visual Concepts, Seattle Washington.

Waves

A WAVE LASTS only moments
but underneath another one is always
waiting to be born. This isn't the Tao
of people but of waves.
As a student of people, waves, the Tao,
I'm free to let you know that waves
and people tell the same story
of how blood and water were born,
that our bodies are full of creeks
and rivers flowing in circles,
that we are kin of the waves
and the nearly undetectable ocean currents,
that the moon pleads innocence
of its tidal power, its wayward control
of our dreams, the way the moon tugs
at our skulls and loins, the way
the tides make their tortuous love.to the land.
We're surely creatures with unknown gods.

JIM HARRISON

From *Saving Daylight*, published by Copper Canyon Press.
Designed and printed by Chris Copley at the School of Visual Concepts, Seattle, Washington.

Ocean

Olav H. Hauge
Translated from Norwegian
by Robert Hedin

This is the ocean.
Vast and gray,
gravity itself.
Yet just as the mind
in solitary moments
suddenly opens
its shifting reflections
to secret depths —
so the ocean
one blue morning
can open itself
to sky and solitude.
See, the ocean gleams,
I, too, have stars
and blue depths.

From *The Dream We Carry*, published by Copper Canyon Press. Designed and printed by Sukhie Patel at the School of Visual Concepts, Seattle, Washington.

Pool

Heather Allen

In a wide and quiet hollow
Where the river slows,
Dark in the shadow of the trees
And amber with the light of stones,

The water turns upon itself, and shifts
Transparent panes above an unknown depth.
Trees overhang
Their images, that seem to rest

Upon the dark leaves on the bottom,
Where twigs and spotted shadows
Turn to fish, and drift
Into the center of the pool to feed—

Their circles widening
Then disappearing,
Like echoes of a sound
Beyond our hearing.

From *Leaving a Shadow*, published by Copper Canyon Press.
Designed and printed by Laura Bentley at the School of Visual Concepts, Seattle, Washington.

JUNE GHAZAL

Arthur Sze

Is the sun a miner, a thief, a gambler,
an assassin? We think the world

is a gold leaf spinning down in silence
to clear water? The deer watch us in the blue leaves.

The sun shines in the June river. We flit
from joy to grief to joy as a passing

shadow passes? And we who think the sun a miner,
a thief, a gambler, an assassin,

find the world in a gold leaf spinning down
in silence to clear water.

From *The Redshifting Web*, published by Copper Canyon Press.
Designed and printed by Danielle Crandall at the School of Visual Concepts, Seattle, Washington.

Late March

A dark day raining.

A bright flash

Of blue jay disappearing

Into black folds

Of a dripping spruce tree.

Bark of ash and apple tree shine

In the dim drizzle.

The woodpecker's song this afternoon

Is a chipping noise,

A sound that puts little dents

In the wet air.

Tom Hennen

From *Darkness Sticks to Everything*, published by Copper Canyon Press.
Designed and printed by Heidi Hespelt at the School of Visual Concepts, Seattle, Washington

SIGNED LIMITED EDITIONS

JIM HARRISON
Dead Man's Float

Jim Harrison (1937–2016) called poetry "the true bones of my life," and published seven collections with Copper Canyon Press. A highly accomplished prose writer, Harrison's legacy also includes the novella trilogy *Legends of the Fall,* the novels *Dalva* and *Farmer,* and the pæan to good food and cooking, *A Really Big Lunch.*

"*Dead Man's Float* is, as its title would suggest, a flinty and psalmist look at mortality and wonder."—*Los Angeles Times*

150 numbered editions. Signed in full by Jim Harrison. Hand-bound by book artist Rory Sparks. Title "Dead Man's Float" blind-stamped onto front cover, with no author name and no spine label. Cover cloth is Green/Gray Millstone.
End sheets are Hahnemuhle Bugra.

$200 Numbered | ~~$500 Lettered~~
sold out

JIM HARRISON
Saving Daylight

250 signed and numbered copies. Davy boards quarter-bound in
brown and burgundy Brillianta cloths with gold-stamped spine.
Handbound by the Watermark Bindery.

26 signed and lettered copies. Davy boards quarter-bound in
Japanese brown silk and gold-stamped burgundy calf leather
spine. Handbound by the Watermark Bindery.

$125 Numbered | ~~$300 Lettered~~
4 copies available   *sold out*

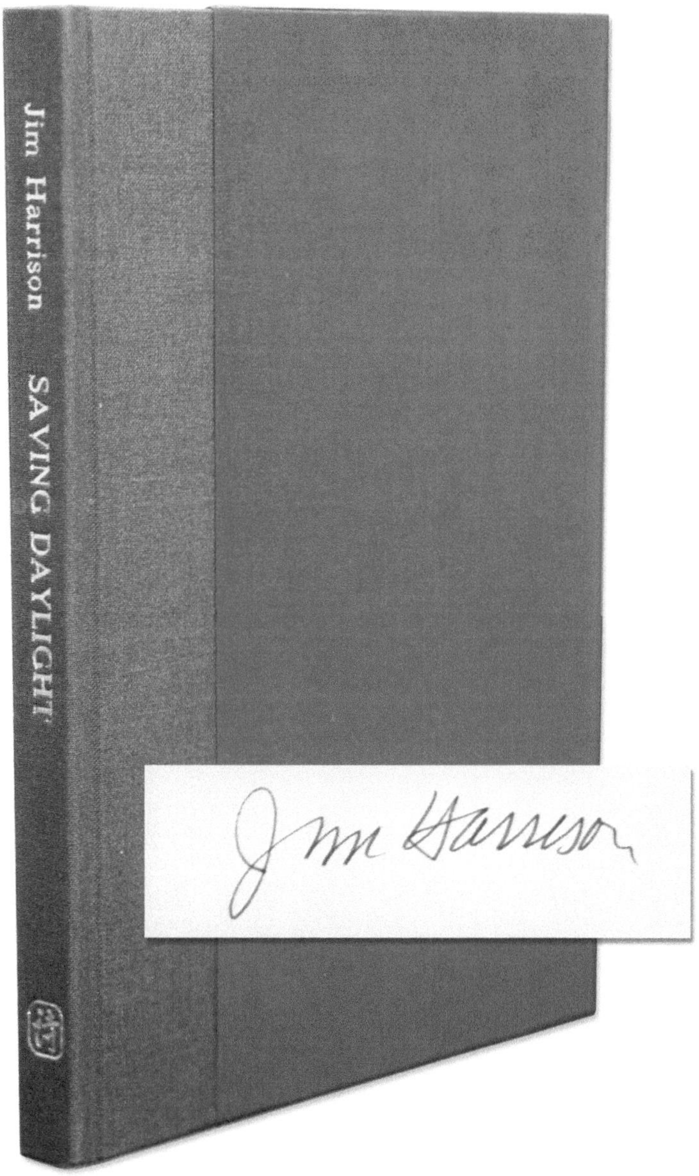
Jim Harrison SAVING DAYLIGHT
Jim Harrison

TED KOOSER
Delights & Shadows

Ted Kooser served two terms as Poet Laureate of the United States, and his *Delights & Shadows* won the Pulitzer Prize for Poetry in 2005. Lauded for the accessibility of his work, he has been noted as the "first Poet Laureate of the Great Plains." A retired life insurance executive, Kooser holds a position as a Presidential Professor at University of Nebraska.

"Kooser documents the dignities, habits, and small griefs of daily life, our hunger for connection, our struggle to find balance in natural and unnaturally human worlds." —*Poetry*

250 signed. Davy boards quarter-bound in green Brillianta cloths with gold-stamped spine. Handbound by the Watermark Bindery.

26 signed and lettered copies. Davy boards quarter-bound in midnight blue Japanese silk and gold-stamped mocha brown calf skin spine. Handbound by the Watermark Bindery.

$75 Numbered | ~~$300 Lettered~~
sold out

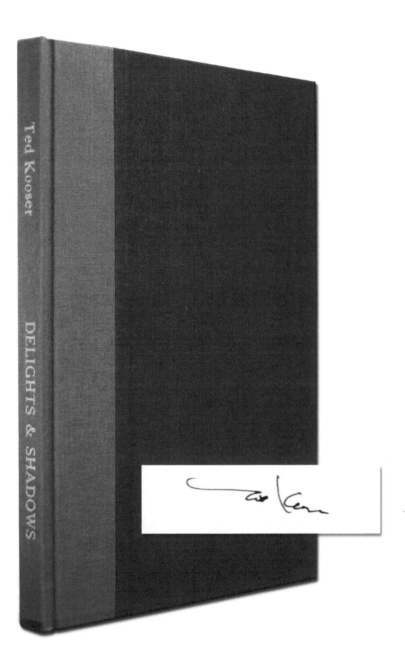

W.S. MERWIN
Garden Time

W.S. Merwin is one of America's greatest poets. He has authored over fifty collections of poetry, translation, and prose. He served as Poet Laureate of the United States, and he has received nearly every major literary accolade this country has to offer, including two Pulitzer Prizes.

In a review of *Garden Time,* Merwin's most recent book of poems, *The New York Times* noted that his work "feels like part of some timeless continuum, a river that stretches all the way back to Han Shan and Li Po."

150 numbered and 26 lettered editions, all signed by the author. Smythe sewn by Gary Robbins and hand bound by Rory Sparks, with a hand-printed Warm Gray Iris book cloth and Hahnemuhle Ingres end sheets. Each lettered edition is enclosed in a beautiful slipcase, which opens with a gate fold and closes with a clasp bearing Gwen Arkin's The Garden House in a tin-type style. Lettered edition includes a letterpressed broadside of *My Other Dark* by W.S. Merwin.

$300 Numbered | ~~$500 Lettered~~
sold out

W.S. MERWIN
The Moon before Morning

100 numbered and 26 lettered editions, signed by the author.
Asahi Black Mohair over boards and hand-bound by Rory
Sparks. Title and author gold-stamped on front cover. Lettered
edition includes hand-printed end sheets and a broadside of
"One Day Moth" housed in a silk sleve. Both end-sheets and
broadside printed by The North Press.

$300 Numbered | ~~$500 Lettered~~
sold out

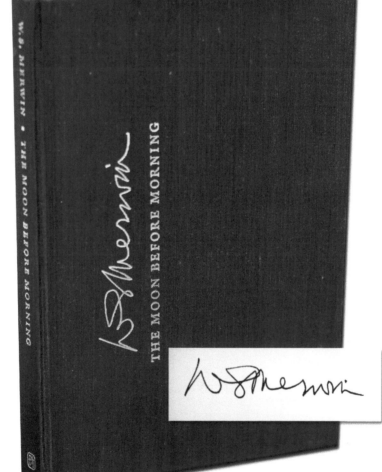

BILL PORTER / RED PINE
Finding Them Gone

Bill Porter, under the pen-name Red Pine, is one of the world's foremost translators of Chinese poetry and religious texts. He has published six volumes translations with Copper Canyon Press, including the bestselling *Taoteching* and *Collected Songs of Cold Mountain.*

Finding Them Gone: Visiting China's Poets of the Past, is a fast-paced pilgrimage with the goal of paying homage to dozens of China's greatest poets by visiting their graves—or trying to—and performing idiosyncratic rituals with small cups of Kentucky whiskey. Illustrated with over one hundred photographs and two hundred classical poems, most of which have never before appeared in English translation.

"Bill Porter has been one of the most prolific translators of Chinese texts, while also developing into a travel writer with a cult following."—*The New York Times*

100 numbered editions. Signed by Bill Porter. Smythe-sewn binding, full leather covers, sewn-in silk bookmark, colored map endpapers. Title blind-stamped on front cover.

$150 Numbered | $300 Lettered
sold out

BILL PORTER / RED PINE

FINDING THEM GONE

RICHARD SIKEN
War of the Foxes

Richard Siken is a poet, painter, filmmaker, and an editor at Spork Press. He is a recipient of the Yale Younger Poets Prize, two Lannan Residency Fellowships, and a Literature Fellowship in Poetry from the National Endowment for the Arts. His second book of poetry, *War of the Foxes,* appeared from Copper Canyon Press in 2015.

"This may be the most anticipated poetry book of the last decade… expect it to haunt you."—*NPR.org*

200 numbered and 26 lettered. All copies signed by Richard Siken. Smythe-sewn binding, silk-screened cloth covers and end-papers. Lovingly hand-made by the imitable Spork Press.

$100 Numbered | $300 lettered

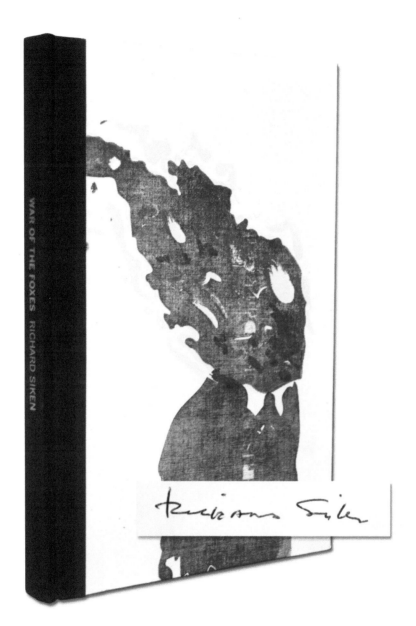

Poetry is vital to language and living. Since 1972, Copper Canyon Press has published extraordinary poetry from around the world to engage the imaginations and intellects of readers, writers, booksellers, librarians, teachers, students, and donors.

WE ARE GRATEFUL FOR THE MAJOR SUPPORT PROVIDED BY:

THE PAUL G. ALLEN FAMILY FOUNDATION

 amazon literary partnership

 the point envision·enact·evolve

 4 CULTURE

 golden lasso

 Lannan

  National Endowment for the Arts arts.gov ART WORKS.

 A& OFFICE OF ARTS & CULTURE SEATTLE

 SEATTLE FOUNDATION

 WASHINGTON STATE ARTS COMMISSION

The Chinese character for poetry is made up of two parts: "word"
and "temple." It also serves as pressmark for Copper Canyon Press.

The book is set in Minion, a typeface designed for digital composition by Robert
Slimbach in 1989. Book design by Jacob Boles. Research
and writing assistance provided by Jennifer Rudsit and Shelley Whitaker.

Special Broadside Offer

All broadsides featured in The Broadside Register are available
directly from Copper Canyon Press while supplies last.

When ordering, use promotional code **BROADSIDE17** to receive a
25% discount on your total purchase. Discount code valid through
December 31, 2017.

Three ways to order:
- Visit www.CopperCanyonPress.org
- Call toll free 877-501-1393
- Mail in the order form on facing page

ORDER FORM

NAME			
ADDRESS			
CITY		STATE	ZIP
PHONE		EMAIL	

SHIP TO (IF DIFFERENT):

NAME			
ADDRESS			
CITY		STATE	ZIP

TITLE	QTY.	PRICE	TOTAL

Subtotal:	
9% sales tax for WA residents	
Shipping: $4.00 for 1st item, 50 cents each additional	
Discount	25%
Total:	

COPPER CANYON PRESS
PO Box 271, Port Townsend WA
98368

877-501-1393 toll-free order phone
360-385-4925 phone
360-385-4925 fax
www.coppercanyonpress.org

Discount valid through December 31, 2017

PAYMENT METHOD: ☐ Check ☐ Money Order ☐ MasterCard ☐ Visa

Card Number [ ][ ][ ][ ][ ][ ][ ][ ][ ][ ][ ][ ][ ][ ][ ][ ][ ][ ][ ]

_____   _____

NAME AS IT APPEARS ON THE CARD   EXP. DATE